Among the Monarchs

CHRISTINE GARREN

The University of Chicago Press
Chicago and London

The University of Chicago Press, Chicago 60637
The University of Chicago Press, Ltd., London
© 2000 by The University of Chicago
All rights reserved. Published 2000.
Printed in the United States of America

20 19 18 17 16 15 14 13 12 11   2 3 4 5 6

ISBN-13: 978-0-226-28410-1 (cloth)
ISBN-13: 978-0-226-28411-8 (paper)
ISBN-10: 0-226-28410-7 (cloth)
ISBN-10: 0-226-28411-5 (paper)

Library of Congress Cataloging-in-Publication Data
Garren, Christine
    Among the monarchs / Christine Garren.
        p. cm. — (Phoenix poets)
    ISBN 0-226-28410-7 (cloth : alk. paper) — ISBN 0-226-28411-5 (paper : alk. paper)
        I. Title. II. Series.

    PS3557.A7177 A83 2000
    811'.54—dc21   99-052850

For Sam, with love

Contents

Acknowledgments

The author would like to thank the editors of the following journals in which some of these poems (occasionally with a different title) first appeared.

The Southern Review: "Small Things," "Love," "First Time," "Picnic" ("There was a clearing of yellow grass . . .") "Solitaire" (appeared as "Tea"), "Landscapes before Surgery," "The Calf" (appeared as "Encounter"), "Figure and Ground"
Ploughshares: "The Biopsy"
The Chicago Review: "Picnic" ("I had packed the bread and apples . . .")
Pequod: "The Underpass," "The Laboratory," "Fortunes"

The author also wishes to express her gratitude to the National Endowment for the Arts for their generous support.

Childhood

From the tree, a swing is hung. A mallet
rests against the fence. And on the lawn, a woman gathers pecans.
I think about her all the time,
partly in disbelief, partly because she is my mother. But now it's dusk.
The light is silver
under the closing sky. The birds sing, rapt in discourse. One
has a thread hung from its beak. The other, the offspring, has a needle.
Its feathers are needles. Its song
is a needle-song.

The Bride

I waited for a long time, long enough that the field trees blossomed.
And the animal, pastured for years, lowered its spine
into the grass and died. The pond turned into a sheet of pollen.
I waited through the spring, and before that I had waited.
And when I walked through the steep grass to see the animal's corpse,
there were no maggots. Just grass and the wind. A purity you can't imagine.
And still, you won't come here with me?
When I keep smoothing out a place beside me on the granite bench?

Early Memory

My mother comes and leans over me. Her face is the room.
As she lifts me, she sings. And I understand,
while a train passes through the edge of Cleveland, that she needs to feel
my need for her. Night fills the window she has walked me toward.
Then she's silent. I understand shapes, the scent of snow on the earth,
her not singing.—
She took me to the window and I looked through its screen—good girl.
Look, now, through the wind, over her grave's stretched tent.

First Time

On Sunday I was in an upstairs bedroom on the bed, being forced.
I saw us on the face of the mirror, the dune of our white flesh.
Afterward, I looked out through the window where it was summer.
The sky was cloudless, and under it vines twisted around the birdbath.
And a bird threw down its image on the grass. I thought of the world
unfolding itself in another country, of another girl's story—
not here, because I knew that God was in the yard,
because the yard was beautiful, and he had stayed
mute among the monarchs.

312

When my mother was dying, I visited her room. I took in some photographs
of when she was young, standing beside my father.
She loved him more than most wives love their husbands.
When she was dying, her body was a balloon of fluid. I was afraid.
The room was hot; its window faced the afternoon sun
in early spring, before the air-conditioning was turned on.
I went back to her apartment and waited. I wasn't there. I wasn't brave.
The fifth time she told me to go away, I went away.

Love

Lorraine might be in the other room writing songs.
On weekends she played at a bar where she waitressed.
Raymond had been in Vietnam, with Vietnamese women.
And now he loved Lorraine who hated him because he was poor
like her parents were. I saw them once, Raymond and Lorraine.
She stood a little higher, on a step, and her face, lit by the backdoor light,
had the keenness of a hawk's—though what I saw one rarely sees
between animals: a belief in doom, a giving in to loss,
which is when they kissed.

Picnic

There was a clearing of yellow grass where a deer ran.
The air was still, and I remember the loudness of my pack's zipper
when I opened it for cloth and bread and a knife.
A blind of leaves hung from the apple tree. And then, when I looked up
to the other side of the meadow
I saw my dead one, my unborn, wearing her dark swamp hair
wave to me from a place on the grass. I did not know
she had gone there with me—and that she would be beside me forever,
as she is now, like an animal, wanting back inside the house.

Monarchs

We sit at the table and talk. It's late and I know I need to leave soon.
Deer will be in the meadows, beside the highway, ready to cross.
I keep waiting for my mother to give me a sign, that it's all right,
I can go. This goes on like a rope back and forth
over a grassless piece of earth: I ask her with a glance, and she responds
not yet.— When I do leave, she stands beside the railing of the back porch
and waves. I blow the horn. We both know what we're doing.
It's like the butterflies for a school project, years ago.
While we pinned their wings to Styrofoam, we talked.

The Analyst

The doctor and I were walking down the path. There was some evening wind,
a few quick birds. And then at some point he touched my hand and said "there,"
when we were stopped before a small pond.
The tips of our shoes touched the black liquid.— He was showing me the truth,
though there was nothing on the face of the water.
I stared into the flat glaze and saw a few gnats, a slight current.
And then I understood—
my form covered the pool.

The Calf

It was dawn and there was still blood on the earth, on the grass,
where the calf had been born. Its mother was moored behind it.
I looked at them both for a long time because their eyes
were like small flats of stone. And when dawn began clearing
the green border, the animals remained full of indifference.
We had been like that: blood had been involved. There was the early-on
fierce energy, the energy of incest, and then, over it all,
a strange indifference—
while I listened to the tight silver motion of the river
and to a plane's heavy passage overhead.

The Skaters

Junipers line the field edge. Now and then there's silence
between the animal calls. One of the bobcats crosses the field.
Then the trees, forked at the base, lead to the bridge
and to the snow figure with pebble eyes, and pieces of rock
fitted for the big bush crotch, and pine cones for breasts. At her base
there's a pool of spilled juice, for menses.
And then the forest gets very dark, enlarging itself—
while the mocking children sleep.

Family

Beyond, the roofs of other houses are at a slant and ashen
as if in an etching. Even then, the world felt like someone else's art.
The geraniums did not seem to come from God. The swings beyond held
     no one.
But my brother and I are playing Hearts with our mother and father,
in the sunroom, before the first one folds his cards away,
then as in our lives: our father first, then our mother—before
my brother and I raised our heads and were, as we are now,
king and queen of the abyss.

The Cemetery

My friend was an artist. She'd use a sycamore stick and draw
a graveyard on the earth. She added footpaths, and the standard
graveyard trees. I made bouquets of leaves for the dead.
All afternoon we made up death-dates for those we loved.
Then she'd smooth the earth with her hand and start again.
Her brown hair guarded the stick she wrote with.—
When my father died in a building near the ocean
and I was floating on a raft in darkness
it happened as she had said it would, years ago,
in the Venn shadow where we played
after school, under the swings.

The Underpass

I walked into an underpass at fourteen. It was summer
and the trees were hot with sun when I went into the concrete shade,
where the river moved under the bridge. Pigeons flew between the cement
    rafters
and I must have stayed for a long time
because when I came out on the other side, it was dim. It was evening.
A black wind paced at my shoulders. The moon had risen, and an elm
    stood
in its new pitch of light. In the underpass, this is what happened:
I was raped, I lost part of my body, my family died, I killed
three of my children. That the moon is here, that I'm able to see it
is testament.

First Love

I took everything off. Sometime in February. For him. For myself.
Snow was on the cement border around the pool
and on the tennis court that was one caged square of dust.
But he, he was dense like a jetty
with a silver east wall of air. Then, he was like
a concussion that I woke up from
but woke up differently. Smaller. A little ruined. For years
unable to speak.

Tristia

I saw birds in the yard. They were silent, like wet leaves on the grass.
And past them, the garden was quiet too. I saw the vines'
thorns, each one
like a small, thick bell. And there was a rabbit
that did not move. Is this the yard we came from? And later I saw the antler
of an animal, though it, too, was paralyzed. And then I saw nothing.
A shutter was pulled over the view. The darkness
was without brevity
as it is now
in your lips.

Solitaire

My love for him? It was like the stone
I saw the cashier wearing once. On a braided rope.
And like the flight pattern of monarchs
over a dune of yellow grass.
It was a fan
in summer. And it was like a piece of gravel
in my windpipe, that still did not stop me from kneeling down or breathing in
enough air to beg for more.— Lifted as if from the sea, opened, under
the sky's hugeness, and thrown back.

Sulfur

Especially on weekend nights, I'd hear the other tenants' cars
on the gravel drive. In between that sound
were the crickets in the black air.
Then I'd hear the voices of couples over their radios. It was summer
when I'd lie beside the open window
in the guest room, while my mother slept across the hall.
Even then, I'd hear her cough, then cough again. Again, the cough.
And then I'd hear her draw
the match across the book.

An Account

The doctor comes in quickly, after you're already on the table.
There's no eye contact or small talk. Sometimes there are ten more to be done
before lunch. So, there's a sense of urgency. The patient tries to please.
A nurse stands near your head, grabs your hand, and then soon enough
it's over. You have your life back again. The pain is in the humiliation.
The gowns have flowers on them. A girlfriend sits in the waiting area,
reading. Later, the fathers put their heads into their hands and weep.

The Tenant

Toward the end of August, I understood I had rented a room
that would never be mine because being in the room
was like standing in the air of an oasis blunt with emptiness.
And I understood something of the couple before me was still there,
that the man had loved the woman
the way a boy loves the dock-girl at the edge of town.
All summer it was like this, though I brought in friends
and rearranged the furniture. It was not until
one evening, when I looked down through the window
into the apple tree full of moths,
that I understood I was in a place of grief.

Noon

Now no one is here. Not even I am here
in full.

The sun
flattens itself against the glass.

And though the room is all mine, it is
a desolate theater.

Everything around me's grave. The bird in the holly
stands in its grave.

Here
is a grave. I remember the other Saturdays

when this room was a field
in Austria. I remember the center of his body—

how I wept and wept.

A Doll's House

When I was born, after the violence, they took me into a room
where they take the illegitimate infants. Later, I was adopted.
I was held by strangers and spoken to with the voice of strangers.
I was loved; I was lucky.
By now, I imagine the woman who gave birth to me is dead.
When I find her grave, the stone is tilted back, for me to see in—and then
I do look into a house where she moves
first from the piano to the kitchen, and from the kitchen
to the side-room, where the television is. Then to the bed, to the bed.
And then the house is dark.

Picnic

I had packed the bread and apples and a knife.
The paths were dry underfoot.
But once there, the dahlia seemed the only thing on fire. Its petals floated
like flames from the attic of a burning house.
And though he moved in closer to me,
like a wall of air from the sea, when I looked into his face
it was still and blank at first—
not without desire—but with
the force of glaciers carving ground.

The Biopsy

When I closed my eyes
I thought about playing tennis with him
a long time ago on the deserted court, a mile from the ocean.
And the rallies that lasted a long time
while the overhead clouds drifted like gulls. I thought not so much about him
as the field of us. The sun-embalmed afternoons, and sleepwalking
for two years under the heavy pin oaks on the way to the pier and fish houses.
And then—and then—
the death of it.

Cedar

The cedar is green again. The snow melted, on the black earth.
The wind bends the tree back and forth—as though it were young—
the wind coming with its blue cave of nothing.
The cedar is the center of the world, arching
with its spine
in the hood of the wind
bending, then straightening and bending again
as if to suggest yearning, as if to express love's
horror and grief.

The Kite

He must have been looking toward the lawn,
to the wide green leaf of it below us, then to the apple tree.
And if a strong wind had come, the leaves
of the apple tree would have been lifted upward, with the tree taking on
the form of a kite,
and he would have seen that the apples are knots in the kite's tail
because if his mind had been less filled with the tree,
if he'd seen my face in its wilderness, he would have understood
what the year had done, and not have touched it.

The Newlyweds

The real story is that she was a piece of light
sleeping on a stone shelf in a shed. And he had come up the hill,
having just fed the dogs, and was seated on a crate
cleaning the mud off his boots, when he looked up and saw her
between the bags of lime, and empty jars, mousetraps,
and ant poison, and the box of nails. And was so moved
by her beauty that he felt his breath reach into the muscles around his kidneys,
then touch his pubic bone, then move
far back against the wall where the mind begins.

Small Things

Through heat paths, the minnow travels

to love and nuzzle
the algae of a stone.

A whole season passes
before fish and granite kiss—and there is

grief
to the minnow.

A silent
boom

in the water. "But I loved!"
And the human, gazing down through the heat paths,

gives it a shadow
to vanish in.

Paperweight

Look at the man and the woman
together on the island, salt on their flesh, gulls over the dunes.
The ocean near the cottage steps. They have walked all day
in shadows thrown by yaupons. Her pockets are shells.
You cannot tell from here that their floor
is fresh snow, that they will eventually
understand
they are there, to be hidden.

Landscapes before Surgery

In the most remote, jungle-like corner of the island
there is the cabin, made of mint, where we lived. Past all the alley-rows
of papayas, beyond
the shed, and tools with teeth. If they want to see more deeply in,
I can show the surgeon
the Japanese-like balance
of the room, and my hips sometimes in his hands
in the cabin made of mint—where I think I must have first become ill,
where the first cell must have divided, somewhere
sometime in that paradise.

The Wolves

At first there was nothing. I saw the hollow cold,
the white plain field, hard with ice. And then, at the edge

I saw the wolves, nine of them, together
as if a single animal.

The weave of their breath hung above their ash-colored coats.
And they stood mouth to flank, shifting in their order—

the work of their veins in the quiet of winter.
Then, what I understood would happen, happened. The door

at the timbered edge, the one they were
to return through,

closed. Lost, their young. Lost, the sheep they planned to eat.
And they had no choice but to turn in my direction.

In the Garden

I used to have desire, all the time, then I remember the exact placement
of the sun when I stopped desiring. The blackbirds were in the vines.
And I heard water running from an outdoor faucet.
A neighbor beyond the fence was speaking in a kind and maternal voice
to the flowers. There was a hammock. I remember the sun upon this,
at its perfect, particular angle, like a blade across the yard.
But I do not remember what happened inside me—
it was quieter than drowning—and like that
it had no breath.

Figure and Ground

In the summer I walked a trail, trying to accept things as they are.
Living among the small things.
For six weeks there was no rain; I took in the bright fields,
then the languid creek where two herons lifted over the water
as if their carriage were itself the air.
But it was God I was talking to now, not because the flowers
had a stricken beauty, but because for the first time
I commanded him, ordered him,
to notice me.

Janus

I had a friend who lived in the country.
Her gray house leaned like a tent in the middle of a field.
And the nearby trees stood like animals gathered in a herd,
their thick trunks a grove of shadow. One afternoon we rode her seesaw
while her father stared from behind the kitchen window.
I realize now he touched himself underneath the sill's beveled plane.
I remember the board, warm with sun, beneath me as we played
in the eastern line of the yard—
and the sound of our feet's etchings on the dry earth
when I looked across and saw her eyes, already haunted.

The Swan

A swan glides across the pond; now and then it forms
a warp in the surface. Without a noise,

the black water holds the hidden rudder. In the pines,

a bird calls out
above the hook of the swan's neck

but the swan only continues
glossing its double, fastened

to the water. Flight would help—to see strain,

or wind to bend the trees, or wind
to drop a needle on its perfect form.

Tree-line

I have a sense of the horizon, of its humpbacked ridge
that, too, leads to an abyss. The dark hums like a hive of bees.
And the sky tilts its dim theater toward me.
This is how the world is, then, alone. Better. Otherwise,
I'd have to listen to your telling me that it is not dark.
Telling me we are not going to die.
We would have talked again about the house and how to fill it.
Now, it's just the stars, barely visible, that blink and blink.

Trout

Sheets over the windows, and there was snow on the ground
when I led him along the path to the house, down a row of stone steps.
I was thinking about wanting the meal to be perfect.
And the bread was. And the trout was tender.
Then we talked about a life near the sea, children, day after day of love,
    youthfulness one can't
imagine ending—that was years ago, before tonight
when I heard the fish spine float
its molecular music in the galaxy of the dead.

The Daydream

I drift. The oar, safe in the oar-lock. From time to time
a figure moves on the bank, between the smoke of a just extinguished fire.
He hammers a stake into the earth for his tent. Then there's nothing
but the heavier sound water has, in its deeper parts.
And I dip my hand into the tree bark's lengthening shadow and wait
while a bird flies into the place where Cepheus will come—
while the universe convinces me
that I've moved into its body.

Solitaire

It is late summer again. At least that's how I remember it.
The shape of your head is like a monument
as you move through the gardens
with leaf-prints on your arms. There's a bridge with water underneath.
Later, I felt the sweat
collect behind my knees in your friend's apartment. Later, I kept on and on
looking at a dove. When it is late summer, I go through this—wanting
the time back, again, because now if I decide to love someone
I turn them away.

Fortunes

"You have a wise spirit; use it generously."
I would enter through the back door that was black and usually bolted,
put on make-up, and my outfit,
then strip. It's funny to me that in the end
it was
my spirit that I got close to, and uncovered, and
was generous with.

"All the troubles you have will pass very quickly."
My room is very quiet tonight. The window is full of wind.
Voices in the street rise up and reach me through the parted curtains
and I see the shaven heads of the young glisten— and it's true,
just seconds ago, there were no troubles.

The Student

My friend has worked for a year now on a painting.
I know the work is about watching westerns while lying in bed
with a man married to someone else. And it's about the scuppernongs
he placed around the carcass of the bird
he cooked for her— that they ate from a tray between them, in bed.
That's why the painting is of an arbor of grapes, and is beautiful,
because if you get up very close you will see that she has added,
in the sunlit netting, the twist of a human form.

Picnic

When the man and woman are finished, they throw the last wings
to the dog. There's an apple in the woman's lap, in her skirt,
in late spring. At some point, in watching her fold the cloth
into the basket, I remember that I am going to die.
The willow leaves sway back and forth as if to show me the earth,
studded with weeds. The trees along the river stand like monks.
I understand the dog, the can of insect repellent, the couple—
their dirty baby that cries and is ignored and then stops.

Courtship

I used to walk a sidewalk in winter. The houses on either side of the street
were poor. The yards dirty
and bald, with small frozen pools under the clotheslines. The sticks
of last summer's flowers stood beside the cinder-block foundations.
Around this was the music of the river. Above this
was the sky on the hill.
I walked everyday. And then one time a figure appeared, at one of the doors,
waving, under the awning.
And I waved back with my life.

Apartment Complex

Someone else sits there now, hearing the children.
It is summer, and by the pool, the gate opens and closes late
into the afternoon. There's a small mound of flowers on the hinge side
of the fence, and the person
before the sliding glass door looks out to the world as it is. I remember
mostly the sounds—of someone coming with groceries through
the complex-corridor, the sound of a paper sack, keys, and a door closing.
Then the voices by the pool again, things of the afternoon, life
as I have not heard it since.

The Ruins

I think I spent my life
lying in the grass, waiting to be touched. And then I was

briefly held. And then I was left alone.

The rest of my life is a matter of return
to being with the wind, with a few lifting moths, the grass,

to the time before

I had felt any passion.— In the summer, in the past,
I would visit and tour the ruins of ancient cities.

Now there's no need,
the dust-flown bits, the broken steps are in me—their clouds

of brevity and endurance.

Warehouse

I've just thought of his hands as they moved years ago
over his laces. I was waiting, holding the joint
for his turn
when I lost the angle of his head as he lowered it
over the difficult shoe. A warehouse stands at the field-edge now,
its aluminum panels
like partitions to a lost world—storage-place
for the drop of saliva I spilled on the ground
and for the thread of clothing left there
and the earring, lost, somewhere near there

and the inability to love anyone else.

The Exercise

I work in silence. The small boat rests halfway on shore, among the reeds.
My mother is in the center seat, waiting. She wants me to lift the bow
and lower all of the keel into the water. It's dark.
And I do this. Quietly. The only noise is of the boat's aluminum, once,
    against a stick.
What follows is a large expanse of lake water, under the stars,
and the sound of the oars as she works them, in their sockets, forward.
The backwash hits the reeds and settles at the cuff of my ankles.
And then it's over. She's gone. The tree frogs speak in the dark.

The Laboratory

I was on the phone late at night, at work. Everyone else had gone home.
Close to midnight, I could see the parking lot, lit with a few lamps,
where one of the workers ran across it, into the arms of a woman. She stood
posed, as if on a gray screen in a theater.
I couldn't believe
his foolishness. Black clouds moved quickly across the face of the moon.
I couldn't believe her ignorance. Then I saw him touch
the door of her wrist
through which they vanished.

Cake

The girl's hand is pressed against the tree. It's early summer
and her skin is still white with winter. Her boyfriend is beside her
and they're laughing; their teeth are like two rows of shells
in the watermelon-colored sunset, years ago. There was the scent
of lighter-fluid and meat and then at last I reach the memory
of cake in between his lips, and how I wanted it, and want it still—
standing beside the fire-escape steps where I live, where the birds lift
into the alley air.